FOUNDATION BIBLE CLUB
A-Z STORY BOOK

'Dipo Toby Alakija

© Copyright 2012 by 'Dipo Toby Alakija

All rights reserved. No part of this book may be reproduced or transmitted in any form or by any means without permission of the publisher.

ISBN: 978 - 978- 49874-2-4
ISBN: 9784987422

Printed in United States
First published in 20012 and republished in 2016 by the publishing house of

CALVARY ROCK RESOURCES

19, Ajina Street, Ikenne Remo,
Ogun State,
Nigeria.

36, Thomson road
Gorton
Manchester
M18 7QQ
United Kingdom

270 Madison Avenue
Suite 1500, New York, NY 10016
United States

www.calvaryrock.org

Dedication

This book is dedicated to every woman who builds her home with diligence, to every man who heads and provides for his family, to the teachers who understand the fact that they design the future of the nation through what they teach the young ones in their classrooms and to all children who are the future of every nation.

THIS LECTURE IS BASED ON THE SEMINAR THAT WAS HELD WITH TEACHERS, PARENTS, MINISTERS, CHURCH WORKERS, SCHOOL PROPRIETORS AND OTHER PROFESSIONALS BY THE AUTHOR IN NIGERIA.

The essence of delivering the lecture in this book is to expose every adult to the fact that children are the future of every nation. How they are designed will determine how the future of their families, communities and the nation will be. Secondly, I hope to inspire as many people as possible to get involved in children work. As a matter of fact, the responsibilities of raising children in the way of the Lord are the responsibilities of everybody. Even if you do not have the burden to train other people's children, you do have the duty to raise the ones God gives to you.

As way of introducing this lecture, I would like to share with you one of the methods the Marxists used to ensure that communism system was established firmly in Russian.

The group of Marxists (followers of Karl Max) always launched her campaign against any form of belief in God through young ones. The Marxists would go into churches and schools and tell children and youths to test two hypotheses and see which one to accept as a theory. One of them is the belief in God while the other is the belief in communism. They would tell the young ones to pray to God to give them biscuits. If he gave them, they could believe there is God. If he did not give them, then they MUST believe that there is no God. The young ones would pray for biscuits but, of course, God never works that way. So there would be no biscuit. The Marxists would go ahead and tell the young ones to ask for biscuits in the name of communism. As soon as they ask for it in that name, some people who had been stationed outside the church or school would start throwing biscuits inside the place. There would be wild excitements. These children would live to be diehard atheists that posed serious threats to any slightest belief in God. That is one of the reasons a typical communist is an atheist.

This story proves that the whole country or generation could easily be programmed through the young ones. This lecture is very crucial to everyone dealing with young minds. It focuses on: (i) Categories of children (ii)Types of Children (iii)Total child and (iv) Building the total child.

CATEGORIES OF CHILDREN

Following the Biblical classification of children in Psalm 78: 4-6, we can categorize children into three which are:

(1) The ones that are yet to exist. Verse 4 of that passage says, "... showing to the generation to come the praises of the LORD, and his strength, and his wonderful works that he hath done." We can see from this passage that the Lord is mindful of children that are not even yet born. One of the greatest problems of this generation is that they make a lot of babies that are not planned for. Children that are not put into consideration while planning for future often constitute nuisances. In fact, when they are teenagers, they become mothers or fathers that would produce other nuisances.

(2) The second category of children is the ones in formation stage. This implies the ones that are already in their mothers' wombs. Some people kill their children before they are born and call the act abortions. Children are being made every minute. Some people that make them consider them mistakes. Many people, unknown to them, have destroyed people that are supposed to be blessings to mankind when they were at formation stage. I read a story of the proprietor of a very prestigious school in America. The man related how his mother attempted to abort him when he was in her womb because he was considered unwanted! The author of the book asked his readers, "supposing the woman had succeeded in getting rid of the baby, what do you think she had aborted?" He answered almost immediately, "a great school!" Children even at formation stage are important. So they must be cared for and put into considerations.

(3) The other category of children are the ones that are already born. These are the ones we want to study so as to know how to build them mentally, physically and spiritually. Let us first study the types of children that already exist before we talk about what makes them total (complete).

TYPES OF CHILDREN

With reference to Tim Lahaye's book titled: Spirit-Controlled Temperament and for the purpose of this lecture, which is designed to teach laymen and to enhance the knowledge of professionals and strictly not for academic purpose, we can divide children into four broad groups. Although, as Tim put it, there could be a blend (mixture) of two or more of the categories in one person. They are: Sanguine (popularly considered as extroverted), Choleric (can be considered to be strong willed personalty), Phlegmatic (can be considered to be reserved person) and melancholy (considered to an introvert). The personalties is not the concern of this lecture. Tim's book is strongly recommended for proper understanding of all categories of people. Our concern in this lecture is the factors that are responsible for the various characters of human beings generally. These factors are what distinguish one person from the other. The factors are as follows:

GENETIC FACTORS: The word GENETIC is borrowed from the medical term Genes. The genes and chromosome are discovered scientifically to be responsible for the character or nature of a person. It is passed from the parents to the offsprings through what is called gene pool that are contributed by extended family, especially all the grand parents. Hence, if the nature of a person is attributed to genetic factor, it would be very difficult, if not impossible to change. In that wise, such person would need to master how to control himself. It is ideal if the person is taught how to manage himself right from his childhood. This is where the next factor comes to play its role.

ENVIRONMENTAL FACTOR: This factor has a lot of influence in the life and character of both children and adults. When talking about influence, I mean the components which a person gathers from different sources to form his life style. A lot of people develop negative attitudes because they pick the wrong person as heroes. Environmental factor implies two things. They are the place and the people. The combination of these two will influence the behavior of an individual. The place a person is raised is very important in character formation. For instance, if someone lives in the desert, he will live to endure the sun and thirst while he who lives in the jungle will learn to kill wild animals if he wants to survive. Similarly, a city boy will behave like a city boy and a villager will naturally behave like a villager. The people in an environment is also important in the character formation of a person since the norms, customs, lifestyles, dressing, language and other things are attributed to the people. If your mentor is a doctor when you were a child, you would like to be a doctor. As teachers, parents and children/youth handlers, we have what it takes to mold and pattern the lifestyles of the children. Whatever we plant into them is what they would play back to us when they grow up. So we must show them only the good and not the ugly side of us. All human beings have both saints and beasts inside them. Let us show them the saints in us. If we show them our beasts, we will develop the beasts inside them.

SITUATION FACTOR: Is what can influence every human being to behave in certain way. It can be described as a prevailing circumstance over the natural disposition of an individual. There are certain situations that bring frustrations, depressions, trauma, complete change of attitude and even mental disorderliness in both young ones and adults. Do you ever observe it in your class a naturally pleasant student suddenly becoming another thing entirely? The child could be going through a trauma that is caused by what is going on between her parents or within the family. By the time you complete this seminar, you will know how to manage a number of complicated problems like that. Now, I don't want you to feel that I have answers to all the problems. No! Nobody has answers to all problems but I believe God have not created what He does not have the power to control.

Having discussed the types of children and factors responsible for their natures in the simplest form, let us now look at the total child in the simplest form as well.

THE TOTAL CHILD

Total child simply means a complete child just like a complete man or woman. What makes a person complete is not whether he or she can produce or not or whether he is normal person or not. What makes a person total (complete) are basically three. They are: (i) The physical being (ii) The emotional or mental being (iii) The spiritual being

The complete person God creates comprises of the body (physical), the soul (emotion) and the spirit. That is to say man is a tripartite being. That means he exists in three parts. The three parts are what makes a person or a child total or complete. Before we discuss each of these parts, I want us to consider a controversial issue, not for the basis of argument but knowledge. The issue is: is everybody in this world a complete person? The truth is: NO! There are some people that are considered humans because they have bodies but they are actually mixture of human and unclean spirits. What I mean by that is that instead of such bodies of human to be inhabited by human spirit and soul which are invisible, they are inhabited by other spirits. Check the story in Genesis 6:1-8 where there was perverted version of the original creation of man. God has to destroy the world just to preserve his original creation by preserving Noah and his family. The story serves as one of my references that prove that not all humans are total. The other references can be inferred from all that has happened and are still happening around us. I would like to link such happenings to what seems like myths in Africa.

In Africa, there is this event about certain women giving birth to children that would live for a short period and die. They call such children Abiku which literarily means child that lives and dies after a short while. If a mother suspects that she has given birth to Abiku, the body of the child is marked with sharp object, often times with the belief that the child would stay alive. In most cases, the children die. When they are born in another time into the same family, they came with the marks on their bodies. This principle is also applicable to the belief in reincarnation that is common in other parts of the world. In reincarnation, it is believed that when a person dies, he comes back again either as another person or as an animal. In such case, the person who claims to have reincarnated is either possessed with the demons who transmit the information about the dead person into him or such person is soulless beings. If it is in the former case, he can be delivered if the demon that possessed him is cast out of him. I have my mother as a case study.

When my mother was young, she claimed that she was not really my grand mother's daughter. She claimed she was actually my grandmother's sister who died before she was born. She was able to convince my grand mother that my great grand mother was her real mother by narrating all the events that happened before she was born and during the life span of the aunty whom she claimed she was. This forced my grand mother to take her to my great grand mother who accepted her as her daughter. After the death of my great grand mother few years later, however, my mother became a Christian and forgot all about her claims. Elderly members of the family were confused that she could not recall any of her claims and proofs she gave them. Her uncle who is still alive as at witting this book was the most surprised that she could not remember a thing. I personally questioned this uncle and my mother about the issue. She has truly forgotten about the claim. In fact, she told me she was scared about the whole issue. I took time to explain to her what was actually happening.

With my findings so far, it is instructive to note that not all human beings in this world are complete. Just as man crossbreeds animals to form another animal, the devils we can not see have been crossbreeding human bodies with unclean spirits since the time in Genesis chapter 6.

Now let us study what makes a person complete.

THE PHYSICAL BEING: Is the part of human beings that can be seen with the eyes or through the use of any equipment like X-ray machines. This part had been studied by man. Hence experts like doctors know how each part of the body structures functions. When there is defect, man knows how to correct it with the use of drugs or other things. When the body wears out, however, the spirit with the soul which cannot be seen would have to leave the body. When that happens, it means the person is dead. Some bodies last long and some does not either as a result of sickness, spiritual or emotional problems. In any case, we live longer than one another. Our bodies need to be taken care of like a property because they house our souls and spirits. It is erroneous belief that when a person dies, he or she reincarnate. The Bible says in Hebrews 9:27 that it is appointed unto man once to die, but after this the judgment. This place makes it clear that once our bodies wear out they go back to the dust, the soul with the spirit do not stay this world. We have enough proofs that indicate that once a person dies, he faces judgment of God.

THE SOUL (OF THE EMOTION): The soul is responsible for the emotional or mental well being of a person. Whatever goes wrong with the soul affects the body. So the soul needs to be fed with right things just like the body. You have probably heard the adage that says that you're what you eat. Similarly, if you feed your soul with the right thing, you will become the right person. If a person is fed with wicked things as in the case of Adolph Hitler, he becomes what people calls "wicked soul." The soul is also responsible for what people call conscience. Conscience cannot die as some people assume but it can be made inactive. Just like the body, soul grows as it is fed with the right or wrong information. The environmental factor can influence the positive or negative growth of the soul through influence of the people in the environment. It is the soul that is responsible for the good or bad things a man does. That is why the Bible says in Ezekiel 18:20 that the soul that sins shall die. The death of a soul is different from the physical death. The meaning of the death of a soul is found in Revelation 21:8 which says, "and all liars... shall find themselves in the lake which burns with fire and brimstone which is the second death." The studies of soul of a man is a complex issue but for the purpose of this seminar, let us view soul as the part of a person that characterizes and distinguishes man from animal through emotion, human conscience, ability to gather and use information, make decisions and relate with others.

THE SPIRIT: is also the invisible and immortal part of a person that makes it possible for him to operate in the spiritual realm. Whether we believe it or not, there is a spirit realm from where what would happen in the physical realm is designed. That is why it is possible for anybody to dream of what would happen before it actually happens. He gets this information through his spirit. It is only through the spirit of man that man can know God. The reason many do not know God despite the works of His hands is that their spirits are inactive. However, it can be made active by influencing the soul through the teaching of the Word of God.

There are lots of things going on in the spirit realm because the Supreme Being - God - is a Spirit and the real enemy of man, the devil is also a spirit. Angels and demons are also spirits. God who created man wants him to be reconciled to Him through Jesus Christ after the fall of man (Hebrew 9:14-17). The devil also struggles to possess the soul of man by trying to control him through unclean spirits. In the spirit realm, God through His Spirit or the devil through various demons is in control of the soul of each person in this world. Some people are under God's control while some are not. Some may be deceived that they are on their own but no one is independent of either of the spiritual controls.

Like in the case of soul, the study of the spirit is also a complex issue. So let us see the spirit of a man as the part that operates in the spirit realm. Let us now go into the next issue.

BUILDING THE TOTAL CHILD

Having studied what we need to know in the total person, let us see how we can build or develop the total child. Please, note here that the three parts are very essential. They are so dependent on each other that you cannot leave out one. For instance, you cannot pass any message to a sick child or emotionally depressed child or spiritually tormented person. There are so many spirit related cases being treated in the hospitals or other places.

There are certain methods that can be applied to develop all the three parts. Let us discuss that first.

TEACHING METHOD: We are not talking of teaching methodology now but teaching the young ones, using materials like books, visual aids and other things. When you teach a child a subject, he or she believes it. At that tender age, they believe virtually everything. He believes that once the adults say it is so, then it must be so. They are yet to possess the intellectual abilities to question what they are taught unless they are faced with facts that conflict it. At that age, they are still gathering information about life and looking for ways to approach it. Teaching method which can be formal or informal is often done orally or in written form. What a person teaches a child goes a long way to affect a generation. If everybody is conscious of what he or she teaches the children, I believe a whole society can be repaired, no matter the state just as the Marxists programmed the country of Russia with communism through young ones.

CONDUCT METHOD: This is done through what the children observe in the environment that is created by the adults. As human beings, they have eyes to watch the conduct of parents or teachers. They have the memory to record what they see and they have other parts of the brain that use the information to act. In other not to stress this part unnecessarily, I will use an incidence that occurred a few years ago in my wife's school. I watched a boy of about five years telling a girl of the same age, "let's do what my father and mother do everyday when we want to sleep." Before anyone knows what was happening, the boy was on top of the girl. I grabbed them and beat sense into the two of them. I invited the mother who is an illiterate and related the incidence to her. What she said proved to me that illiteracy is worse than a disease. She said, "it's not my fault. It's my husband who always pull my..." Please, don't let me tell you that part.

ENTERTAINMENT METHOD: This is also a way of passing messages in form of entertainment like music, movies, story books etc. What most people do not realize about this method is that it is the most effective method of passing both negative and positive messages. Many countries, especially in Africa are influenced by the western world through movies and music. The world is easily deceived through entertainment. A boy in Abeokuta shot his friend dead with his father's gun while trying to imitate his hero in a drama. A lot of children have turned violent because they pick violent people as their heroes or heroines in a fake world - the movies.

INFORMATION METHOD: This is a way of sharing facts that is often backed with proofs like pictures, visual aids and other items. A typical example of this is found in documentary programs or videos like the testimony of a man that died and was preserved in the mortuary, coming back to life after four days. The film is titled "Raised from the Dead." Often times, information method is required to convince people of so many things, including spiritual things.

The above are the broad methods that can be used to build or develop the three parts of a child. Let us now discuss methods that may be peculiar to each part.

The physical being: can be developed through proper diet, physical exercise, observation of health and safety regulations. If there is defect in the physical being, the ideal thing to do is to see the doctor.

The soul: Apart from the three methods mentioned above, the soul can be developed through what some people call "wilderness experience." The human body has no way of recalling previous hardship once it is comfortable but a soul that is well developed through hardship can. The soul of a man can grow into maturity through meditating on the word of God. Please read Psalm 1:1-2

The spiritual being of a person: Apart from the other three general methods, this area can also be developed through prayers and sometimes fasting. In 1 Thessalonians 5: 17, the Bible says, "pray without season." This is because, according to 2 Corinthians 10:4, the weapons of our warfare are not carnal, but mighty through God to the pulling down of strongholds." We read in Ephesians 6:12. that we wrestle not against flesh and blood, but against principalities, against powers, against rulers of darkness of this world, against spiritual wickedness in high places."

In conclusion of this lecture, I want to distinguish the roles of schools which primarily focus on the physical and mental or emotional aspects of a child from that of the school Bible clubs which focus on the spiritual aspect. Although this book attempt to put the academic aspect into serious consideration but the major concern is the spiritual development. Other volumes of this book which is expected to be used for each year would all be available. Please, if you want to maximize the use of all the six Foundation Bible Club story books, please, study the design, usage and special notes below.

THE DESIGN OF THIS BOOK

Although this book is designed to entertain, edify and teach the children of all age groups the way of life as commanded by God in the scriptures; it can serve academic purposes in schools, Churches, homes and other places. The Bible lessons, rhymes and songs demand certain levels of understanding of the scriptures, literary skills and creativity. It is an enormous job for parents and teachers to maximize the use of this book. I therefore crave for the indulgence of anybody who wants to use it to study each material with the Bible diligently before using it to teach others.

CHILDREN BETWEEN 0 - 2 YEARS: This age group can be best stimulated with only songs. They may be taught the letters from A to Z and the Biblical representations. If the teacher is not familiar with the suggested tune for any of the songs in the book, he or she would need to use another tune. Besides, he or she would need to learn many more songs apart from the ones in this book. The rhymes may be formed into songs and sung to the children regularly. If children in this group hear the songs often, they will unconsciously learn it by heart as they grow up.

CHILDREN BETWEEN 3 - 6 YEARS: Before they reach this category, the children would have probably learned all the letters in English Language and perhaps their representations. It is, however, advisable to repeat the lessons so that they can be familiar with the pronunciations.

Also the spellings of the representations of each letter may be introduced e.g. A is for Angel. Spelling of angel: a- n- g- e- l. The children will need to learn the rhymes by heart and the portion they are to memorize at this stage.

CHILDREN BETWEEN 7 - 10 YEARS: At this age, the children are expected to begin to appreciate the lessons in the story. A more literary aspect of the rhymes can be introduced to them. They can be taught what makes a good rhyme. Rhyme simply means the ends of two or more words sounding the same or similar. For example, the rhyme about an angel takes this form:

A is for Ang - el
Who can always t - ell

The end of Angel and Tell sound similar, so they rhyme. Similarly, the end of each word of the rest of the verse rhyme.

Of the danger a - head
Whose wings spr - ead
Over my little head

Apart from this, there are some literary implications of most of the rhymes in this book which may demand certain Bible knowledge and poetic insight of the teacher. For instance, to explain the rhyme of Angel in a very simple way for a child in this group, it may be explained like this: " Let us give letter A to Angel who is capable of knowing when and where there is going to be danger. Because he is a messenger from God, he knows all things. He is always around to guide and protect a (little) child like me against any danger ahead." It has taken 49 words to explain the rhyme of just 19 words. Of course, it can be more elaborate than this, especially if it is juxtaposed with the Bible. That is what most of the rhymes and poems are all about. Saying so much with very few words.

Children in this category can read and understand the stories although it is necessary for the teacher to retell them as he teaches the Bible lessons in each story and ensuring that they appreciate the importance of the portion they are to memorize. They also need to be made to understand the implications of each Bible lessons in each story by attempting the comprehension test.

CHILDREN BETWEEN 11 YEARS AND ABOVE: Young one in this category is expected to appreciate the deep meaning in the rhymes, sing or compose the songs and understand the messages in the stories with the use of biblical principles. Some of the stories are like the parables Jesus told his disciples in the Bible. For instance, in the story titled "The marriage of the prince," we can see the Prince as Jesus; the place of party as this world that is full of sins. The slave is the sinner that becomes born-again and the time the slave was taken to the palace, which is heaven as the Second Coming of the Lord. There are other lessons in some stories like "The Robber" which need to be interpreted with the Bible. Since the songs are based on the general Biblical principles about ways of life, they are meant for them to appreciate. The more sense the teacher can make out of the rhymes, the songs and the story, the more knowledge he can pass to the students.

Also at this stage, they can attempt the comprehension tests, write their own or dramatize stories, compose music or poems and rhymes in the book.

THE USAGE OF THIS BOOK

INDIVIDUAL USAGE: This book, just like the rest of Foundation Bible Club Story books, is packaged with the hope that the lessons inside would be shared with others. So it can be used by individuals to establish Bible Clubs or Children Fellowships at homes and other places. The materials can be used also to minister to youths and even adults. Although most Christians are yet to see the need to be involved in sharing the word of God but the question they must ask themselves is: "what can I do for the Lord for all He has done for me?" The Lord had used other people to reach out us. Hence, we must also reach out to others. This reminds me of the twin sisters whose parents are ministers of God. They attended a big and old school that was established by a man who did not believe in God. Many people who passed through the school died as atheists. It was thus difficult to share the gospel in the place. The twin sisters could not tell anybody about Jesus in the school even though they have been told in the Church that it is important to share the word of God with everybody. They came across the old edition of this book which so inspired them that they decided to share with their friends the stories inside at recess period. They were able to attract all their friends with the stories. It soon became the habit of many of the students to gather in one place to hear stories from the book. Before the teachers got to know what was happening, the twin sisters have formed a Bible Club where they could sing songs in the book, hear stories and even worship God in the school that was established by an atheist! And guess what. The school decided to let them do what they desired since they meant no harm.

If ten year old children can form a Bible club with some of the contents in this book in an atheist's school, no Christian has reasons to say he or she cannot do it. Considering the years of preparing all the stories in the books, I believe God wants individuals to use them to create a platform to worship and share the word of God with young ones everywhere, including their homes.

ACADEMIC USAGE: There are activities that are designed for academics for almost all the categories of children. The pictures that need to be coloured by young ones are meant to give them the idea of what they are to learn when they grow older. The stories and the comprehension tests are for older children. The teacher needs to mark each assignment so as to monitor their progress in the lessons.

The book is also relevant in creative and literary environment because most of the 26 songs, 26 rhymes and 26 stories create rooms for drama, musical presentations, literary and poetic insight at the elementary stage; motivating students to become writers, dramatists, poets and singers. All these may be considered as elementary literatures which arguably are pure academics.

CHURCH/FELLOWSHIP/BIBLE CLUB USAGE: As this book is specially packaged to edify the total person in individuals, the materials are to be used to minister to young ones in primary and junior secondary schools and churches. Going by the testimonies and reports I received from Bible teachers, parents and ministers, the books have helped them to create and effectively managed Bible Clubs in schools and at homes, equipping the children departments in Churches with edifying materials. Please, see the notes below if the book is to be used for these purposes.

To conclude these areas, I have to admit that the suggested ways to use the books are not the best. They are just to assist those who are not really familiar with this kind of teaching materials. I am sure people who have more teaching experience than me would have a better method. Let us use your idea or mine and then allow God to give us the increase.

SPECIAL NOTES FOR BIBLE CLUB TEACHERS AND CHILDREN MINISTERS

This book is expected to be used every week through out the first year of establishment of Foundation Bible Club in primary, junior schools or children departments in the Church. Hence it is advisable to maximize its use by injecting some special programs like literary debate which can be developed from some of the comprehension tests, dramatizing some of the stories and composing the songs or the rhymes into songs in between the weeks of the year the story book is to be used. All these task the intelligence of young ones, motivate them to acquire the knowledge of the word of God, boost their moral values and develop their talents in music, drama and creative writings, improving their communication skills and creativity. There may be need to set examinations for them at intervals, using the comprehension tests and the lesson notes as a guide. There is also need to constantly review what the students have previously studied before they study the next lesson. It is also essential to give room for the students to have a forum for discussions and contributions during the fellowship each week.

If you are just starting Bible Club in the school or at home, the programs below which are typical of the ones Calvary Rock Resources have helped to establish in schools can serve as your guide.

1. Praise and worship
2. Opening prayers
3. Revision of the previous lessons.
4. Special number or song or drama presentation if any.
4. Story and Bible lessons in the story of the week
5. Class activities
6. Prayers
7. Offering for the fellowship if the school permits. (The offerings are used to acquire teaching materials or used to organize special programs for members of the school Bible Club each term.)
8. Closing Prayers

Please, note that this is not a rigid program. It can be adapted to suit time or environment of the school or location.

Since the above is just a guide, I believe the Lord will assist whoever wants to use any of the story books to influence young ones. Calvary Rock Resources could be informed through the address of the publisher if the school or church needs help of our missionary team or copies of this book or the next volume. The organization can also be informed if there is need to train their workers on Children Evangelism And Missionary works.

Letter A a

A is for Angel

Can you trace and colour this angel?

RHYME ABOUT ANGEL

A is for Angel
Who can always tell
Of the danger ahead
Whose wings spread
Over my little head

SINGING BIRD WANTS TO TEACH YOU A SONG ABOUT ANGEL

If you want to sing my song first sing the song titled "He's got the whole world in His hand" and use the same tune for my song.

He creates the angels
In heaven
He created everything
In this world
He created you and me
In this world
Jesus Christ is the Creator

MEMORIZE THIS:
God created everything in the world, including me.

LESSON NOTES IN THE STORY BELOW
1. There is evil and danger everywhere in the world. (Psalm 91: 5-6)
2. God protects everybody that believes in Jesus. (Psalm 91: 2-7)
3. Children of God must not be afraid of anything. Instead, they should pray and trust in God to help them. (Psalm 91: 5-16)

ANGELS ON MY GUARD

Once upon a time, there was a little boy in West Africa called Mark. He was an obedient child of God who did all he read in the Bible. He always prayed and sang songs of praises to God.

One day, as he was going to school, two dreadful looking men kidnaped and took him to a witch doctor called Babalawo. Of course, the Kidnappers were going to sell Mark to him for rituals. When they got to his place, Babalawo said to the two men that Mark was different from the people they have brought to him in the past.

Mark who was filled with the Spirit of God said, "I'm a child of God. That's the difference. My father will send his angels to fight with you if you don't let me go."

Babalawo snorted. He asked, "who is your father?"

"Jesus is my father," Mark replied with confidence. Babalawo looked angry as he took one magic ring in his pocket, wore it and hit Mark on the chest with it; expecting him to fall down. Of course, nothing happened to him.

Babalawo and the other men looked surprised. He hit him again. Still nothing happened. There were two huge angels around but no one could see them. They stood by each side of the boy, using their wings to protect him.

God made Babalawo and the two men to see the angels. Guess what they did. They flew like birds.

"If you don't take me back to my school, I will tell Jesus to fight with you?" Mark shouted at them.

The two men quickly went back to him. They were afraid the angels would strike them dead.

They took Mark back to school.

COMPREHENSION TEST
1. What is the lesson in the story about Mark?
2. What made Mark different from other people?
3. Why do you think we need angels to protect us?
4. Now close your book and recite the memory portion and the nursery rhyme.

Letter B b

B is for Bible

colour the table

RHYME ABOUT BIBLE

B is for Bible
Lying on the table
Telling God's mind
To renew my mind

SINGING BIRD WANTS TO TEACH YOU A SONG ABOUT BIBLE

Can you see me? Before you sing my song, you have to trace and paint me with any colour of your choice. When you do that, sing the song titled "Rock of Ages" and use the tune for my song.

I will read my Bible
If I want to grow in Christ
I must obey what I read
If I want to live for Christ
I will always preach the word
So that souls may come to Christ

MEMORIZE THIS:
The Bible is the word of God which I need to read everytime.

LESSON NOTES IN THE STORY BELOW
1. All children of God must always read the Bible (Psalm 119: 9-12)
2. All children of God must also tell others what God says (Psalm 119: 13)
3. If you believe what the Bible says, you will experience miracles. (Palm 119: 17-19)

LOLA AND THE BIBLE

There was once a little girl in Nigeria called Lola. After she gave her life to Christ, her parents bought her a new children Bible. She never bordered to read it. She just put it on her reading table and read other books.

One day, she became so sick that she had to stay in the hospital for many days. The doctors and the nurses did all they could to make her well but the ailment became so serious that she thought she would soon die.

"Oh, Lord," she prayed, "please, don't let me die. I want to take care of my parents when I grow up."

Her friends from the school and the Church came to visit and pray with her.

One of them called Dotun read a passage in the Bible to her in Psalm 118:17. "I shall not die, but live and declare the works of the Lord."

"Did God say I will not die?" Lola asked quickly.

"Of course, yes," Dotun replied. "God will still use you to talk to others about Jesus. So you will not die."

"I was thinking I would soon die," Lola confessed.

"Oh, Lola, if you have been reading your Bible; you will easily know when the devil is talking to you."

"So if I don't die, I'll get well?" Lola asked.

"Of course, you're going to get well."

Dotun said, "God has promised us many things in the Bible including good health." Guess what happened. Lola began to pray, using what she has read in the Bible to talk to God. She soon became well. From that day on, she always read the Bible.

COMPREHENSION TEST
1. What are the two things you learnt in Lola's story?
2. What does the passage in Psalms 119:9-18 tells us to do?
3. What is the meaning of (i) declare (ii) ailment (iii) health?
4. Recite or sing the song about Bible

Letter C c

C is for Child

Colour the child and her umbrella.

RHYME ABOUT CHILD

C is for child
Born so mild
He loves and sings
To King of kings

SINGING BIRD WANTS TO TEACH YOU A SONG ABOUT CHILDREN

Can you colour me with green? When you do that, sing "Jesus loves all the children" and use the tune to sing my song.

I am one of all the children
That are precious to Jesus
Whether yellow, black or white
We are precious in His sight
Jesus loves all the children
Of the world

MEMORIZE THIS:
Jesus loves me so much that He takes my pains.

LESSON NOTES IN THE STORY BELOW

1. You may come from a family with so many problems but God can get you out of the problems. (1Chronicles 4: 9 -10)
2. You need to pray and have faith in Jesus before God can help you. (Hebrew 11:1- 6)
3. You must not give up hope. Instead continue to pray and work to become a better person. (Psalm 130: 1-8)

THE CHILD OF SORROW

There was a child in the Bible called Jabez. He was born when his parents had nothing. They could not buy all the baby things he needed. They had to sell all their valuables before they could provide him with food. Jabez always fell sick until his mother got tired and called him a child of sorrow.

When Jabez began school, all the people in the town had to donate some money before his parents could send him to school. Jabez was so dull in the class that if the teacher asked him, "one plus one equals to what?" He would say eleven. So Jabez had to repeat classes many times. By the time he finished his primary school, he was old enough to finish secondary school. Again, he repeated so many classes that when he completed his secondary school, he was old enough to be a father. He could not go to the university because he was so dull. So he started looking for job. But no one was ready to give job to a dullard like him. He could not get a job. So he could not eat anything good.

One day, as he was going with sorrow, he met a man who told him about Jesus. He asked if Jesus could help him out of his problem. The man said, 'yes, of course. If you call on him today, he will answer you.'

Jabez got home and called on Jesus to help him and make him the richest man in the town. Guess what happened. God gave Jabez work as an apprentice tailor. From there he got his own business as a tailor. The business grew into a big tailoring company. Soon, Jabez became the richest man in the town just as he had prayed.

COMPREHENSION TEST
1. What did you learn in the story about Jabez?
2. How was Jabez's life changed?
3. What is the meaning of (i) valuables (ii) apprentice (iii) provide?
4. Close your book and recite the rhyme.

Letter D d

D is for Danger

Can you colour the bones and the fire?

RHYME ABOUT DANGER
D is for Danger
The danger in hell
Jesus' birth in manger
Shows the way to tell
He died for sinner
And gets him out of hell.

SINGING BIRD WANTS TO TEACH YOU A SONG ABOUT DANGER

If you want to sing my song, first sing the song titled "I will make you fishers of men" and use the same tune for my song.

There is danger ahead of you
If you live in sin
And refuse to change
There is danger ahead of you
Unless you repent
Unless you repent
Unless you repent

MEMORIZE THIS:
You must born again before you can go to heaven.

LESSON NOTES IN THE STORY BELOW

1. God's children will go to heaven when they die while all sinners will go to hell according to Revelation 21: 1-8)
2. Anybody can become a child of God if he or she believes in Jesus Christ and stop committing sin. (John 3: 15-20)
3. God does not remember the sins of anyone that becomes a born-again Christian. (Jeremiah 31:34)

THE DANGER IN HELL

Once upon a time, there were two boys called Victor and Banali. Both of them used to tell lies, steal, fight and even disobey their parents.

One day, a pastor went to their school to tell them about Jesus. He said, "there is danger in hell for those who never give their lives to Jesus. You must not tell lies, you must not steal, you must obey your parents and you must not fight anybody if you want to go to heaven."

Victor became born-again that day but Banali refused to change. He continued to steal until he grew into a man. He later died and found himself in front of an angel who showed him how he lived his life. Then the angel said, "Banali, you have done so bad. So you must go to the lake of fire where other sinners are." He was taken to hell where fire burns him. He cried and cried but nobody listen to him.

Victor who was now born-again became old and died too. The angel also showed him how he lived his life. Guess what he saw. He saw only all the good things he had been doing in the book of life. God has removed all the bad things he had done in the book when he gave his life to Christ. So the angel allowed him to go to heaven.

COMPREHENSION TEST
1. What is the lesson in the book of Revelation 21:1-8?
2. What happened to all the bad things Victor had done when he gave his life to Christ?
3. Close this book and sing the song about danger.
4. Recite the nursery rhyme about danger.

Letter E e

E is for Enemy

Can you trace and paint this unseen enemy into ugly looking creature?

RHYME ABOUT ENEMY
E is for Enemy
That roars like a lion
Because I'm a champion
He can't touch me

SINGING BIRD WANTS TO TEACH YOU A SONG ABOUT ENEMY

If you are not familiar with the tune of the song titled: "I love that Man of Galilee", you might have to find another tune for my song by yourself. Before you do that, I want you to colour me with yellow and red.

I love that man of Galilee
For He has fought with
All my enemies
He has forgiven me
All my sins
And makes me overcome
My foes
I love that man of Galilee.

MEMORIZE THIS:
Greater is He that lives in me than he that is in the world.

LESSON NOTES IN THE STORY BELOW
1. Rebellion or disobedience to the word of God makes a person to lose his position in the kingdom of God. (Isaiah 14: 12 - 15)
2. Lucifer, the devil and his servants brought the problems they caused in heaven into the world. (Revelation 12:7-9)
3. Jesus came into the world to make as many as believe in Him the children of God and to give them power to overcome the devil and his servants. (John 1:12, Mark 16: 16-18)

THE ENEMY OF GOD.

So many years ago, there was an angel in heaven called Lucifer. Lucifer used to lead all other angels to sing songs of praises to God. Then one day he said to himself, "I want to be like God. I want other angels to praise me too." So he gathered some of the other angels and got ready to fight with God. God is too big to fight what He created. So He told another angel called Michael to lead other angels to fight Lucifer and his servants. There was great war in heaven as Michael and the other angels fought and defeated Lucifer and his servants. God threw Lucifer with his servants out of heaven and changed his name to the devil and Satan. His servants are called demons, evil spirits and devils.

When God formed the world and made Adam and Eve to rule over it, the devil found a way to take it from them. He succeeded when he made Adam and Eve to disobey God. Since that day, the devil and the demons always bring trouble into the world through sins.

God later sent Jesus to come and give everybody that believes in Him the power to defeat the devil and the demons. That is why Christians use the name of Jesus to command the devil.

COMPREHENSION TEST
1. What was the work of Lucifer and other angels before the war in heaven?
2. What happened after Lucifer had been defeated?
3. What did you learn in the story about the enemy of God?

Letter F f

F is for Fruits

Paint the basket and the fruits with different colours

RHYME ABOUT FRUITS
F is for fruits
With many roots
Given by Jesus
To everyone of us

SINGING BIRD WANTS TO TEACH YOU A SONG ABOUT FRUITS

I don't have a tune for my song. You have to help me find a tune for it. Before you do that, I want you to trace and paint me with your favorite colours.

He is a great provider
Jesus provides the fruits
And provides the food
He created every fruit
All over the world

MEMORIZE THIS:
Always give thanks to God in everything.

LESSON NOTES IN THE STORY BELOW

1. All children of God must learn to give thanks in all things even if they have problems (I Thessalonians 5:18)
2. God has a way of providing for all His children (Philippians 4:19)
3. God can use anything, including animals, man and even angels to deliver those who trust in Him out of evils or troubles. (Psalm 91: 9 - 16)

THE FRUIT AND THE MONKEY

There was a boy in Africa called Eric. He was a child of God who loved to read the Bible. He used to go to church, hear the word of God and even preach to his friends in the school.

One day, he went to farm with his father to cultivate the ground for planting. As he was working on the farm, he saw an antelope. He told his father.

His father said, "run after it!"

Eric ran after it, throwing his cutlass at it. He ran from one bush to another, looking for the antelope until he could not find his way back to his father. He tried to find the way but he could not until it was too dark. He began to cry, feeling hungry and afraid that there might be some dangerous animals around. "What if a lion comes to eat me like a piece of cake?" he thought. Then he remembered what his teacher in the church had said. "Every problem," his teacher had said, "is a chance for us to see that Jesus has the power to save and deliver."

He was hopeful as he went to sit under a tree. He began to sing songs of praise. God touched a monkey that was sleeping on top of the tree to hear Eric's voice, making him to feel so angry that he went to throw some fruits at Eric.

Eric took the fruits and ate them, praising God the more. The monkey felt angry the more. Because it wanted him to stop the songs, he threw all the fruits he had at him and Eric ate everything.

God protected little Eric until a hunter found him. The hunter later took Eric home.

COMPREHENSION TEST

1. What did you learn in the story?
2. How did God feed Eric in the bush?
3. What is the meaning of (i) cultivate (ii) dangerous (iii) deliver?
4. Close your book and recite the rhyme.

Letter G g
G is for God

Can you paint the picture of Jesus and the people with beautiful colours?

RHYME ABOUT GOD

G is for God
Who spoke the Word
That came into the world
He shed his blood
For the whole wide world

SINGING BIRD WANTS TO TEACH YOU A SONG ABOUT GOD

Before you sing my song, I want you to colour me with yellow, red and green. Then sing the hymn titled "Amazing Grace" and use the tune for the song. If you don't know the song, get someone to teach you or you get another tune for it.

My Lord, Jesus!
Though You are God,
You came to dwell with us!
I was full of sins
But you save me
I was in darkness
But now I'm in light

MEMORIZE THIS:
Jesus is Lord forever and ever.

LESSON NOTES IN THE STORY BELOW
1. Jesus is The Word that God sent to create the world and to redeem everybody from sins (John 1: 1-15)
2. The devil was able to take the world from Adam and Eve when they disobeyed God. (Genesis 3: 1-13)
3. Everybody needs Jesus in their lives otherwise the sins in this world would take them to hell. (Romans 6:23)

JESUS IS GOD IN THE FLESH

So many years ago, when God was about to make the world, it has no shape and was full of darkness. There was Someone inside God called "The Word". God said, according to Genesis 1: 3, "let there be light." The Word that was inside God came out through His mouth and went to create the light. It took The Word the whole day before He completed the work. He went back to stay inside God. For six days, God sent The Word to do all the work. On the seventh day, God rested because The Word has done so much work.

When God finished creating the world through "The Word," He saw that everything was good. So He gave everything to Adam and Eve to control.

Now Lucifer who is now called the devil was watching God creating the world. Remember Lucifer in the story titled "The Enemy of God"? If you do not remember, read it again in page 34.

Lucifer wanted to rule the world by all means. So he caused Adam and Eve to disobey God. Since the day they disobeyed God, everybody began to commit sins. Because of this, Lucifer was able to rule the world; making the people to draw away from God. And God became so angry that He said, "anybody that sins shall go to hell." But He loved us so much that He didn't want us to go to hell. Guess what He did. He sent The Word to become a baby in the womb of Mary. When the baby was born, He was called Jesus Christ, the Son of God. When Jesus grew up, He began to tell people to turn away from sin. He became the Savior of the world by dying for our sins. He rose up from the dead and becomes our Lord of all flesh.

COMPREHENSION TEST

1. How did God create the world?
2. How was Lucifer able to rule the world?
3. What did God do after saying, 'anybody that sins shall go to hell'?
4. Close your book and sing the song about God.

Letter H h
H is for Heaven

Can you imagine the beautiful city of heaven? If you can, try to paint this picture with beautiful colours.

RHYME ABOUT HEAVEN

H is for Heaven
The beautiful Haven
Home of the people
That follow the Bible

SINGING BIRD WANTS TO TEACH YOU A SONG ABOUT HEAVEN

If you are not familiar with the tune of the song titled: "My Jesus today", you might have to find another tune for my song by yourself. Before you do that, I want you to colour me with orange and green.

I belong to Jesus
He will take me to heaven
He has built me a mansion
He will not let me down
I belong to the Lord
He will not leave me
Untill we see in heaven

MEMORIZE THIS:

No sinner will go to heaven.

LESSON NOTES IN THE STORY BELOW

1. Heaven is a place of joy while hell is a place of horror in the lake of fire. (Revelation 21: 2-8)
2. The death of a child of God is like a beautiful sleep that makes him or her forget everything about this world. (1 Thessalonians 4: 13 - 18)
3. It is very important that all children of God tell others about Jesus so that they do not go to hell when they die. (Ezekiel 33: 7-11)

HEAVEN IS A BEAUTIFUL PLACE

There was once a child of God in New York called Tope. She loved God so much that she always obeyed him.

One day, she dreamt that Jesus came to take her to heaven. She did not know how she would go there until she fell sick and died. Now don't be sad. When a child of God dies, he or she is going to heaven whether old or not.

When Tope died, she found herself in a city that is made of gold. You are right if you think the city is heaven. There are many angels in the place.

She saw many people who served God before they died in the place. Guess what they were doing. They were singing songs of praises to God like this:

    Thou hath worthy

Thou hath worthy, oh Lord
To receive glory, honor And power....

Tope joined them in singing praises to God, enjoying herself and feeling so happy that she forgot where she has come from.

Then Jesus went to her and said, "Tope, my lovely child, you are too young to be here. I want you to go back into the world and tell the people about this place."

"Oh, no, Lord," Tope said. "I don't want to go back. I like it up here. Don't take me back there, please, Lord."

"Tope, if you don't go back and tell people about heaven, many will die in their sins and go to hell. Do you want them to go to hell?"

Of course not! No true child of God would like anyone to go to hell. So Tope came back into the world.

She soon became well and she started telling everybody about Jesus and heaven.

COMPREHENSION TEST
1. What did you learn about heaven in Revelation 21:4-7
2. What did you learn in the story about Tope?
3. Why did Tope refuse to come to back to the world?
4. Sing the song about heaven.

Letter I i
I is for Idol

Can you paint this idol so ugly that the idolaters would be ashamed to call it their god?

RHYME ABOUT IDOL
I is for Idol
That looks so dull
It's taken as a god
But we know it's a doll
And not the real God.

SINGING BIRD WANTS TO TEACH YOU A SONG ABOUT IDOL

My song needs the tune of the song titled "What a friend we have in Jesus". It may seems a little tough to sing but you can. So let's sing it.

What connection do we have with idols
Which cannot deliver from sin?
We don't have anything to do with them
We are secured in Jesus Christ
I wonder what people see in idols
We must show the real way
For they don't know the way to heaven
The Lord will give the grace.

MEMORIZE THIS:
Anything that takes the place of God in your life is an idol.

LESSON NOTES IN THE STORY BELOW
1. Nobody can serve God and idol. (Matthew 6: 24)
2. God is a jealous God. (Exodus 20: 4 - 5)
3. God wants all sinners to repent and come to Him(Acts 3:19)

THE IDOL TOWN

There was once a town that was full of different idols. The idols were regarded as gods. There was the god of rain, god of thunder, god of cure, god of fertility and so many other gods. All these idols like god of iron and thunder were once human beings. Before they died, they were full of powers of the devil. So when they died, the people carved their images and turned them into idols they would worship.

God was very angry with this idol town and caused no rain to fall for many years. You know, if there is no rain there will be no food because plants will not grow.

All the people in the idol town began to call on their gods, thinking they would bring rain. But the idols are not the real God. They were idols that were made of iron or stone or wood.

Then God sent a pastor to tell them about Jesus. He called all the people to bring all their idols to him. He told them that if any of them was able to bring rain, then it must be the real God. Of curse, none of them was able to bring rain. He said, "If I called on the real God and He gives you rain, would you give your lives to Jesus and burn all these idols?"

All the people agreed. Then the pastor prayed that God should send down the rain.

Then almost immediately it began to rain. All the people were very surprised. They believed that all their idols were not gods after all. So they burnt them and began to worship the real God that sent down the rain.

COMPREHENSION TEST:
1. What does Psalm 115:4-8 say about idols and the worshipers?
2. What is the meaning of (i) thunder (ii) cure (iii) fertility?
3. How did the pastor tell the people about the real God?
4. Close your book and sing the song about idol.

Letter J j
J is for Jungle

RHYME ABOUT JUNGLE

J is for Jungle
Where we can stumble
We know we must strive
In the jungle of life
If we are humble
We will survive

SINGING BIRD WANTS TO TEACH YOU A SONG ABOUT JUNGLE

To sing my song, you will need the tune of the song titled "Give me that old time religion". Before you sing the song, colour me with yellow, red, green and red.

The world is made of jungle
We're all living in jungle
We need Jesus to lead
The Lord led Paul and Silas
He led Mary and Martha
We need Jesus to lead

MEMORIZE THIS:
With patience and obedience
I will get to heaven.

LESSON NOTES IN THE STORY BELOW
1. The way to heaven is very narrow but the way to hell is wide. (Matthew 7:13-14)
2. The enemy called the devil plans to destroy children of God. (1 Peter 5:8)
3. Only children that obey the Word Of God, the Bible will get to heaven (Colossians 3: 16-17)

SHEEP IN THE JUNGLE

There was a shepherd who was taking some sheep to a very beautiful city where they would not feel any pain or hunger. The shepherd had to lead them through a jungle that was full of wicked wolves. The wolves did not want the sheep to get to the city. So they decided that they would either steal or kill them.

The wolves went into the midst of the sheep, pretending to be part of them. They lured some of the sheep away from the shepherd. They took some poisonous food and went to give it to the rest of the sheep. Some sheep ate it and died while some did not.

As they were going through the jungle, the wolves whispered into the ears of some of the sheep, "this jungle is too tough for you to pass. Why don't you take the way that is not rough?" Some who listened to them took another way and missed the way to the city.

Only few sheep were able to get to the beautiful

city.

This story means a lot of things. The jungle is this world and the shepherd is Jesus. The sheep are the born-again Christians while the wolves are the devil and his servants. The wolves that pretended to be sheep are the sinners that pretended to be Christians. They are also bad friends. The poisonous food is sin while those who ate it are Christians who later commit sin. Those who find the jungle too tough are those who stop being Christians because they can no longer follow the word of God. And the beautiful city is heaven.

COMPREHENSION TEST
1. Explain what jungle, wolves and sheep mean in the story.
2. How did the wolves steal or kill the sheep?
3. What did you learn in Psalm 23:1-6
4. Sing the song about Jungle.

Letter K k
K is for Key

RHYME ABOUT KEY

K is for key
The name of the Lord
Given without a fee
To all in the world

SINGING BIRD WANTS TO TEACH YOU A SONG ABOUT KEY

My song needs the tune of the song titled "Prayer is the Key." It is common only in Africa. If you don't Know the tune, sorry, you might have to find another one. Before you sing it, please, colour me with green, brown and orange.

Prayer is the key)   2ce
Prayer will open any door
Jesus gave me the key
And taught me to open
Prayer will open any door

MEMORIZE THIS:
The name of Jesus is the key that opens any door.

LESSON NOTES IN THE STORY BELOW
1. Prayer can be used to perform miracles. (Act 12: 1-10)
2. God answers prayers. (1 Samuel 1: 13 - 20)
3. God always saves everyone that calls on Him, (Psalm 55: 16)

PRAYER IS THE KEY

There was a man in the Bible called Peter. He was a servant of God who preached the gospel to the people in the town. The king of the town called Herod hated Christians so much that he killed many of them.

One day, Herod captured Peter and put him in the prison, planning to kill him as he had killed other Christians. He put some soldiers to keep watch over him so that he would not escape from the prison. When other Christians in the town heard that Peter had been kept in the prison, they began to pray for him. As they were praying, Peter was sleeping. Do you know why? He was tired. He wanted to die and go to heaven to rest.

As he was sleeping, God sent an angel to get him out of the prison. Guess what happened. All the chains the soldiers had used to tie him fell off from his body. Then the doors of the prison began to open without anybody touching them. The angel led Peter out of the prison without any of the soldiers knowing what has happened.

Peter went to those who had been using prayer to open the doors of the prison for him to get out.

After telling them how God got him out of the prison, Peter escaped from Herod, the terrible king.

COMPREHENSION TEST:
1. How did God answer the prayer of Christians that were praying for Peter?
2. What did Herod plan to do to Peter?
3. According to Acts 12:1-19, what did Herod do to the soldiers?

Letter L l
L is for Light

Can you guess what I am? You are right if you say I am a candle. Can you make me easy for everybody to know me? Paint me and the light on my head with red, yellow and other colours.

RHYME ABOUT LIGHT

L is for Light
Shining in the world
Jesus is the Light
He is the Word
And God's Delight
Who died for the world

SINGING BIRD WANTS TO TEACH YOU A SONG ABOUT LIGHT

I use the tune of the song titled "Do something new in my life" to compose this song. If you don't know the song, you have to find another tune. Before you sing it, colour me with yellow and pink.

Send down your light
Through your word
Let your light shine
In my life
Send down your light
Through your Word
Oh, Lord

MEMORIZE THIS:
I am made the light of the world. Therefore, let no man trouble me.

LESSON NOTES IN THE STORY BELOW
1. God can turn the enemies of His children into their friends. (Proverb 16:7)
2. Those who want to live for Jesus Christ should expect persecution. (2Timothy 3:12)
3. Jesus always deliver His people from all kinds of problems. (2 Timothy 4: 18)

THE LIGHT OF GOD

There was a man in the Bible called Saul. He hated Christians so much that he used to beat and throw them inside prison.

When he was young, he was one of those who assisted other people who also hated Christians to keep their clothes while they stoned Stephen, a very good Christian to death.

When Saul became older, he got permission from the leaders of the people to go from one house to another, dragging anybody that was a Christian into prison. At that time, it became difficult to be a Christian because when Saul got to know about it, the person would be in a big trouble. So all the Christians were scattered all over Judea and Samaria. Guess what they did. They still continued to preach the word of God. Saul moved from one town to another, looking for Christians he would take to prison. When he came near a place called Damascus, a light from God suddenly shone. Saul fell down on the ground. Then a voice came from the light, saying, "Saul, why are you troubling me?"

Saul said, "Are you the Lord?"

The voice replied, "I am Jesus, whom you have been fighting." Can you guess what later happened? You are right if you think Saul later became the Christian who also preached about Jesus to everybody.

COMPREHENSION TEST
1. How did Saul trouble the Lord?
2. What is the meaning of (i) assist (ii) drag (iii) permission?
3. How did Saul meet Jesus?
4. Close your book and sing the song about light.

Letter M m
M is for Mountain

Can you colour the sky and the mountains?

RHYME ABOUT MOUNTAIN
M is for Mountain
Which none can move
With might and main
Except by God's move

SINGING BIRD WANTS TO TEACH YOU A SONG ABOUT MOUNTAIN

My song needs the tune of the song titled "Deep And Wide." You can sing it, can't you?

Great and huge
Great and huge
There's a mountain
Looking great and huge

Great and huge
Great and huge
That kind mountain
Can never make me fear

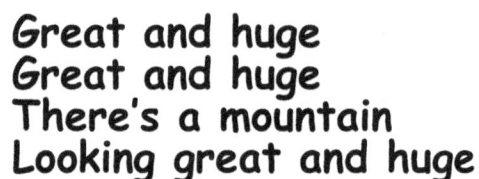

MEMORIZE THIS:
Talk to God about your problem instead of complaining about it.

LESSON NOTES IN THE STORY BELOW
1. If you hold unto the Word of God, God always fulfil His promise to His children. (Romans 4:16)
2. God always lead His children out of temptation. (Matthew 6:13)
3. Whatever a child of God is going through in life, he or she has the strength to overcome it. (1 Corinthians 10:13)

MOUNTAIN OF TROUBLE

There was a little girl called Ronna. Her parents were very poor. They were always in need of money and food.

One day, Ronna's mother fell so sick that she looked as if she would die unless she was taken to the hospital.

Ronna's father could not get money to pay in the hospital. So he went to borrow some money from a rich man called Shylock. Shylock was so greedy that he didn't want to lend Ronna's father some money unless he promised to pay double of the money.

"Apart from that," he said, "you must give me Ronna to stay with me until you are able to pay everything."

Ronna's father agreed because he did not want Ronna's mother to die. Shylock gave him the money and Ronna's mother was treated in the hospital. She became well but Ronna was already with Shylock who would not let her go until her father paid all the money he owed him.

Ronna became so sad that she always cried. She thought of her father and mother who prayed to God to give them the money to bring her back home.

One day, as she was crying under a tree in Shylock's house, a prince who was travelling with his men saw her. He called her and asked, "What's wrong with you?"

Ronna told him what happened. The prince later paid Shylock his money and set Ronna free from him. She went to her parents who were very happy to have her back. From that day, they never stopped praying and praising God for all he has done for them.

COMPREHENSION TEST
1. What is the meaning of mountain of trouble?
2. Why did Ronna's father borrow money from Shylock?
3. Sing the song about mountain.

Letter N n

N is for Night

RHYME ABOUT NIGHT

N is for Night
The time of the Lord
Because we are light
We shine in the world
This is the night
The Lord will come

SINGING BIRD WANTS TO TEACH YOU A SONG ABOUT NIGHT

I use the tune of the song titled "From east to west, I know there is no other God" to compose this song. If you don't know the song, sorry, you have to find another one. Before you sing it, colour me with blue, black and red.

From day till night
I know God is by my side
From night till day
I know God will
Never leave me

MEMORIZE THIS:
I will not be afraid even if I am in danger for the Lord is with me always.

LESSON NOTES IN THE STORY BELOW
1. Spirit of fear does not come from God but from the devil. (2 Timothy 1:7)
2. God does not want us to be afraid of anything. (Joshua 10:8)
3. God is with all His children, no matter what they face. ((Isaiah 41:10))

THE NIGHT BIRD

There was a boy called John. He has three big sisters who were always full of fear.

One day, their parents travelled out of the town; leaving the four children to sleep all alone at home.

At night, there was a great storm and heavy wind that made the trees to rustle and make noise like whistles. Suddenly, there was black out everywhere. It became so dark that no one could see.

John's big sisters became so frightened that they sat still like dummies, feeling as if they were in great danger.

After a while it began to rain heavily. A night bird called owl could not find a place to hide in the rain. So it flew inside the house and began to move from one place to another, making a lot of noise that frightened the girls the more. The owl could not find a comfortable place to stay. So it continued to make noise. One of the girls began to cry with fright, "oh, mummy, daddy, something has come to kill us!"

John who did not know what to do remembered what they had been taught in the church that they must not be afraid of anything. Jesus is always with all children of God. He stood up to get torch a light but one of his sisters screamed at him, "don't go anywhere! Something is there to kill us!"

"Nothing can harm us because Jesus is with us," he said and went to get the torchlight. When he got it, he switched it on and then realized that it was a bird that had been troubling them.

COMPREHENSION TEST

1. What did you learn in Psalms 27:1-6?
2. What made John not to be afraid like his sisters?
3. Sing the song about day and night.

Letter O o
O is for Oil

Can you colour the bottle of oil?

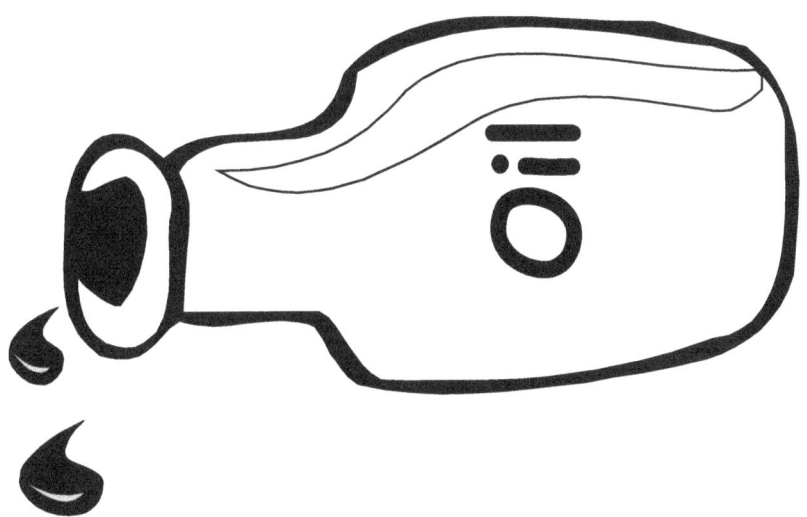

RHYME ABOUT OIL
O is for oil
Which cannot spoil
Filled in my lamp
Given by the Lamb

SINGING BIRD WANTS TO TEACH YOU A SONG ABOUT OIL

I have no tune for my song. So you've got fo help me find a tune for it.

I have some oil
Filled in my lamp
I will never allow the oil
To dry in my lamp
I will never allow evil
To put out my lamp
I have some oil
Filled in my lamp

MEMORIZE THIS:
My life is a light for people to see in the dark

LESSON NOTES IN THE STORY BELOW
1. Jesus would come back into the world to take His people at the time no one expects. (2 Peter 3:10)
2. All children of God must be filled with the Spirit of God that would make them live holy life. (Ephesians 4:30)
3. All Christians must always be ready to meet with Jesus. ((Matthew 44:24)

THE LAMP WITHOUT OIL

There were ten ladies in the Bible called virgins. They were all invited to a wedding ceremony where each of them was to bring a lamp that would give light for them to see.

Five of the ladies were wise enough to have extra oil in the bottle in case the one in the lamp ran out. The other five did not take any extra oil with them. Before the bridegroom came, the ladies have run out of oil in their lamps. So they asked the wise ladies to give them some. The wise ladies refused to give them because they might not have enough for their lamps. So the other ladies went to buy it in the street. But before they returned, the bridegroom had come and the door had been locked. Of course, nobody opened the door for them.

This story means a lot. You can interpret it with the Bible. The oil is the Holy Spirit that helps us to shine. The lamp is the word of God according to Psalm

119:105. The ladies represent the Christians and the wise ladies are those who allow the Holy Spirit to guide them. The other ladies allow the Holy Spirit to leave them because they are careless. They go into the street, which is the world. The bridegroom who is Jesus comes unexpectedly and takes those who are filled with Holy Spirit with Him, leaving those who in the world behind.

COMPREHENSION TEST
1. Why do you think five of the ladies were locked outside?
2. Interpret the story about the virgins with the Bible.
3. Sing the song about oil.
4. Close your book and the song about oil.

Letter P p

P is for Prince

Pain this Prince with beautiful colours

RHYME ABOUT PRINCE

P is for Prince
The Prince of peace
He gave me a kiss
And called me His

SINGING BIRD WANTS TO TEACH YOU A SONG ABOUT PRINCE

> Sorry, I don't have a tune for my song. Would you kindly give it a tune, please? Before you do that, paint me with your favorite colours.

There is no other prince
As Christ
There is none besides Him
Neither is anyone
Like Prince of peace
There is none
Holy as the Prince

MEMORIZE THIS:
To dress decently is part_of godliness.

LESSON NOTES IN THE STORY BELOW
1. To be a child of God, you must be different from people of the world in everything. (1 Peter 2:11, 1 Thessalonians 5:22)
2. God wants all His children to dress decently. (Philipians 4:5)
3. God is closer to people who are sobber or broken than those who are not. (Psalm 34:18)

THE MARRIAGE OF THE PRINCE

There was a king who wanted to get his son a wife. So the king invited all the ladies in the town to a party where the prince would pick the lady he would marry. All the ladies in that town went to the party except a slave who was made to work from morning till night.

All the ladies dressed so gorgeously that the venue of the party was full of colour. Some ladies put on different kinds of bogus clothes and make-up that made them looked like Jezebel. Some put on indecent clothes that irritated the prince. All of them thought they could attract the prince's attention with their dresses.

When the prince was called to pick the lady of his choice, he went round to all the ladies. Of course, he didn't like the way all the ladies appeared. So he went into the street to look for the lady that would be his wife.

As he was going, he heard a beautiful voice of a lady singing: I surrender all Unto Thee, my blessed Savior...

It was the voice of the slave. She was washing her master's clothes. Of course, she was not dressed like the ladies in the party. She was dressed very decently.

The prince went to the slave. As soon as he saw her, he said to himself, "I am going to marry this lady."

She stopped working and fell on her kneels when she saw him. The prince told her he would come to take her as his wife later. When the slave told other ladies what the prince said, they all laughed at her. They stopped laughing when the prince came for her as promised.

COMPREHENSION TEST
1. What is the meaning of (i) gorgeous (ii) irritate (iii) indecent?
2. Why do you think the prince loved the slave?
3. What is the lesson in book of Matthew 22:1-10?
4. Sing the song about the prince.

Letter Q q
Q is for Queen

Please, colour this queen

RHYME ABOUT QUEEN
Q is for Queen
Who is so keen
To be with the King
He is coming
To take the queen

SINGING BIRD WANTS TO TEACH YOU A SONG ABOUT QUEEN

My song needs the tune of the song titled "His Name is higher than any other names." It is common only in Africa. If you don't Know the tune, sorry, you might have to find another tune. Before you do that, please, colour me with blue and brown.

The queen is waiting
She is waiting for the King
The King from heaven
He is coming soon

MEMORIZE THIS:
Whatever you do in the_secret will be made known.

LESSON NOTES IN THE STORY BELOW
1. Whatever a person does in the secret shall be revealed to everybody. (John 7:4)
2. Everybody will get the reward of what he or she has done, be it good or bad. (Matthew 16:27)
3. Always reveal the truth to others, especially when you know someone else is going to be punished if the truth does not come out. ((Isaiah 5:20))

THE QUEEN AND HER ENEMY

There was once a queen who was kind and very intelligent. Because she has the Spirit of God that gave her wisdom and knowledge, she helped the king to rule the town. Most of the people in the town loved the queen except a maid that worked for the king in the palace. She wished she was the queen.

One day, she decided that she would make the king drive away the queen and then she would become the new queen.

She sneaked into the king's room while everybody was sleeping. She took the king's ring. As she was going out, a servant saw her and followed her as she went to hide the ring in the queen's room.

The servant went to take the ring and waited till the time the king would start looking for it.

The next day, the king began to look for the

ring. The maid went to the king and lied that she saw the queen going to take it in his room. The king called the queen and asked her if she had taken his ring. She said she didn't take it. The maid said, "but I saw you take it. I saw you hide it in your room." The king ordered that the queen's room be searched with the maid. Of course, they could not find the ring. The maid was confused and wondered, "Who took the ring?" Then the servant who took the ring went to the king and told him what the maid tried to do. The king sent the maid out of the palace and rewarded the servant for what he did.

COMPREHENSION TEST
1. What did you learn in the story?
2. What is the meaning of (i) intelligent, (ii) keen (iii) sneak?
3. How did the maid plan to become the queen?
4. Close your book and recite the rhyme

Letter R r
R is for Robber

Can you paint this man so ugly that people would be ashamed to be a robber?

RHYME ABOUT ROBBER
R is for Robber
Who is not sobber
Robber starts as liar
And ends in fire

SINGING BIRD WANTS TO TEACH YOU A SONG ABOUT ROBBER

My song needs the tune of the song titled "In the house of God, hallelujah, joy!" It is common only in Africa. If you don't Know the tune, sorry, you might have to find another tune. Before you do that, please, colour me with green, yellow and blue.

You must take offering
To the house of God!
You must take your tithe
To the house of God!
If you use the offering
You are robbing God!
Do not use your tithe
For another thing!

MEMORIZE THIS:
Every robber robs his soul of eternal life.

LESSON NOTES IN THE STORY BELOW

1. It is easy for children of God to rob God by not paying their tithes and offering. (Malachi 3:8)
2. Anybody who does not give to God cannot get His blessings. (Malachi 3:10)
3. Those who rob God must change their ways if they do not want God to curse them. (Malachi 3:9)

THE ROBBER

A man broke into another man's house and took all his money and properties.

The robber began to spend all the money the way he liked. Soon all the money vanished. So he began to sell the properties before he got more money to lavish. Again, the properties vanished. He sat down and thought of what to do. Guess what he did. He went back to the man he had taken his money and properties and began to plead with him, saying, "please, Sir, can you give me some money? I'm so broke."

The man said, "how can I give you my money after you robbed me of my money and properties the other time?"

The robber looked confused and wondered. "When did I rob you of your money and properties, Sir?"

"Get out of my house," the man said. "I will not give you any money. Instead I will curse you to be so poor that you'll not get enough to eat."

Now you may wonder at this type of story. The robber in the story is the person who never pays his offerings and tithes, which is ten percent of all his earnings to the church. The man that was robbed in the story is God. If the person that never pay his tithes and offering goes to God for anything, God will not bless him. Instead, he will become poorer.

COMPREHENSION TEST
1. According to Malachi 3:8-12, how can a man rob God?
2. What happens to anybody that robs God?
3. Recite or sing the song about robber.
4. Close your book and sing the song about robbing God.

Letter S s

S is for Student

RHYME ABOUT STUDENTS

S is for Students
Who learn to be presidents
They are full of sense
Of God's presence

SINGING BIRD WANTS TO TEACH YOU A SONG ABOUT STUDENTS

My song needs the tune of the song titled "You cannot hide it from God." You can sing it, can't you?

We are all Bible students }2ce
Although we are ready
To learn so many things
But we'll never take heresy

MEMORIZE THIS:
Never do in secret_what_you cannot do_in the open.

LESSON NOTES IN THE STORY BELOW
1. Children of God must not be enticed to commit sins. (Proverb 1:10)
2. Children must always preach against sins instead of taking part in them. (Ephesians 5:1-7)
3. God sees everything everybody in this world does. (1 Peter 3:12)

THE NAUGHTY STUDENTS

Martins was one of the few students that fear God in his school. So he always invited everybody to the School Bible Club.

One day, two of the students went to him during the break time and said, "We'll follow you to the Bible Club if you can follow us to where we are going."

"Where are you going?" Martins demanded.

"You will see the place when we get there," they replied. And so Martins followed them without knowing where they planned to go.

The place was a nearby orange farm. The students always went there to steal some of the oranges. When they got to the farm, they told Martins to watch and inform them if anyone was coming while they get busy plucking ripe oranges.

It was when the two students have climbed the trees that Martins realized that they have come to steal oranges! He became very confused. He did not know what to do until God dropped an idea into his heart.

Suddenly, he shouted, "someone is watching us!" Guess what happened. The two students jumped down from the trees and fled like birds.

Martins later went to join them in the school and told them, "you cannot run away from the person that is watching us."

The students asked him, "who is the person?"

Martins said, "it is God. He is everywhere, watching everything we all do even in secret."

The two students later joined the Bible Club where they were taught how to become good Christians.

COMPREHENSION TEST:
1. What did you learn in the story about the students?
2. What is the meaning of (i) attend (ii) demand (iii) realize?
3. Recite or sing the song about student.
4. Close your book and sing the song about students.

Letter T t

T is for Teacher

Can you colour the teacher?

RHYME ABOUT TEACHER

T is for Teacher
That knows the truth
He is the maker
Of future leader
He has the fruit
For molding character

SINGING BIRD WANTS TO TEACH YOU A SONG ABOUT TEACHER

To sing my song, you will need to use the tune of "Sweet Jesus, how wonderful you are." Before you sing my song, colour me with purple and black.

Dear Jesus)2ce
Send down our Teacher
We know Him to be the Holy Ghost
We need Him
To guide us
And to teach us in all other things
We are helpless
So helpless without Him

MEMORIZE THIS:
Teaching the students the right thing is a lasting legacy for them.

LESSON NOTES IN THE STORY BELOW
1. Children of God must have dreams of what they want to become in life. (Act 2:17)
2. If young ones do not have visions about their lives, things may go wrong in their future. (Proverb 29:18)
3. Children need to be influenced to go in the right way (Proverb 22:6-12)

THE TEACHER

There was once a teacher called Miss Benson. She loved teaching young ones in the school and in the church. She would teach them about the word of God and how they could become great. She would say, "I have a dream. My dream is to make your dream come true. If you don't have a dream, I want to give you one. I want you to dream that you become a doctor or an engineer or a lawyer or a nurse or an accountant or a Minister of God. I will teach you all you need to know before you begin to realize your dream and I will tell you what you must not do if you want to become great."

Miss Benson would teach the young ones many things in their books and in the Bible. Soon, all the young ones started dreaming of becoming great in future. And they worked so hard for it.

One day, one of the students went to Miss Benson and said, "I want to be greater than any of the students in the school."

"That's great!" Miss Benson said. "I love that."

"I'll tell you the person I think is the greatest of all."

"Who?" Miss Benson asked quickly and curiously.

"I think you're the greatest," the student said, making Miss Benson to look puzzled. "You're the giver of dreams. Without you, nobody will think of becoming great. And I would like to be just like you, the great giver of great dreams."

Miss Benson was so happy to hear this from the young pupil that she hugged her.

COMPREHENSION TEST
1. What did you learn in Proverbs 4:10-15?
2. What do you dream to become when you are older?
3. Recite or sing the song about teacher.
4. Close your book and sing the song about teacher.

Letter U u
U is for Uniform

colour these people and their graduate uniforms?

RHYME ABOUT UNIFORM

U is for uniform
Of righteousness of God
You need to be reformed
To be a child of God
Be well informed
And turn to God

SINGING BIRD WANTS TO TEACH YOU A SONG ABOUT UNIFORM

Sorry, I don't have a tune for my song. Would you kindly give it a tune? Before you do that, colour me with blue, black and pink.

Christian uniforms
Are made from their holiness
And their garments
Are made from their righteousness
They can be made muddy
If they live in sins,
Disobey the Lord
And refuse to change

MEMORIZE THIS:
Always share what you have with needy people.

LESSON NOTES IN THE STORY BELOW

1. Children of God must always feel concern for one another. (Galatian 6:2)
2. Children of God must learn to give to others. (2 Corintians 9:7)
3. God always reward faithful giver. (2 Corintians 9:6)

THE SCHOOL UNIFORM

Once upon a time, there was a boy called Alan. He was a good boy. He loved to make friends. He had only one school uniform that was so old that it easily tore off. He told his parents about it but they had to save money before they could buy him a new one. While waiting for his parents to save enough money to buy another school uniform, Alan suddenly stopped moving around with other students in the school. He would be the first to come to school and he would not leave his seat until everybody had gone home. Can you guess why? If you think it was because he didn't want anybody to laugh at his uniform, you are right.

There was another boy called David. He is a child of God who loved to make everybody happy. He noticed that Alan no longer played with other students. So he decided that he would cheer him up. David told him about Jesus and how He wanted everybody to be happy.

"I will tell you why I'm not always happy if you promise not to tell anybody," Alan said.

"I won't tell anybody," David promised. Then Alan told him about his old school uniform that was torn. Guess what David did. He went to tell his parents at home that he would like to give his second uniform to his friend who needed it in the school. His parents gave their permission to do that. He took and gave it to Alan. Alan was so happy that he told his parents. His parents came to thank David in the school and that made the principal to hear about it. Can you guess how God rewarded David for his kindness? Well, David was awarded the best student in the school that year. He was given a brand new bicycle by the parents and teachers association of the school.

COMPREHENSION TEST

1. According to Matthew 25:33 - 46, how can you give cloth to Jesus?
2. What did you learn in the story?
3. What is the meaning of (i) cheer (ii) reward (iii) award?

Letter V v
V is for Vegetables

colour all these vegetables

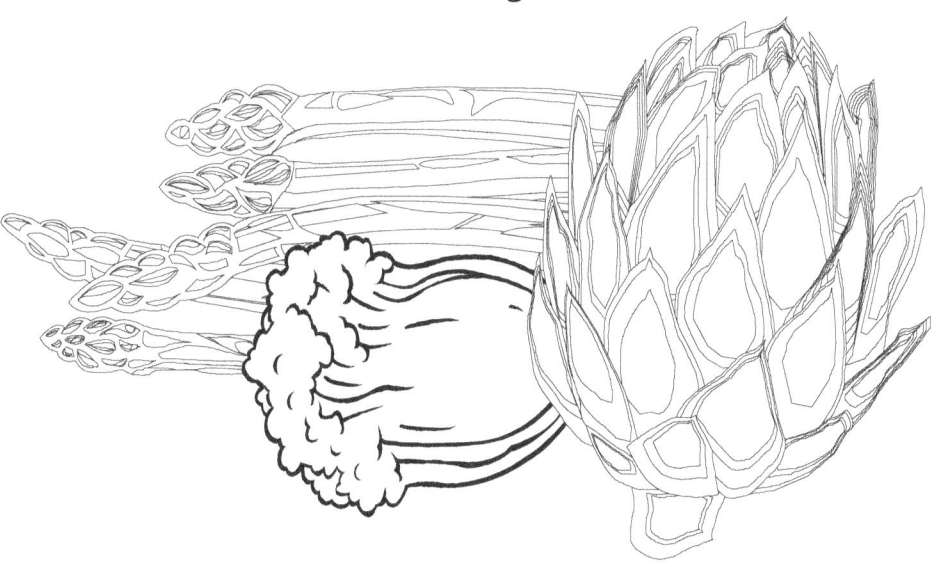

RHYME ABOUT VEGETABLE

V is for vegetable
That nourishes the body
Sit at the table
For food is ready

SINGING BIRD WANTS TO TEACH YOU A SONG ABOUT VEGETABLES

My song needs the tune of the song titled "I will never, never go back to the world."

My Lord Jesus Christ
Created everything
He made vegetables
So that we can enjoy
His work

MEMORIZE THIS:
Never delay what you can do today till tomorrow.

LESSON NOTES IN THE STORY BELOW
1. Children of God must not be lazy. (Proverbs 30:25 - 28 and 6:6-11)
2. Children of God must obey their parents. (Colosians 3:20)
3. There is time for everything in life. (Ecclesiastes 3:1-5)

THE VEGETABLE AND THE MONKEY

Blessing was a member of a Bible Club in one school in Africa. She had been taught to always offer her parents helping hand anytime there was need for it.

One day, she went with her mother to the farm to get some vegetable which the family would eat. They worked so hard on the farm that by the time they got all the vegetables they needed, Blessing was too tired to walk back home. She said, "Mummy, I wish there is a car that would take us home. I feel so tired that I feel like sleeping for a week."

Her mother smiled at her and said, "anybody that sleeps even for a whole day is sick. Anyway, when you see everybody eating the vegetable, you will see that you have not worked for nothing."

"Mum, can we rest before going home? I'm tired."

"Alright, all right," her mother said. They went to sit under a tree where a monkey sat. It got down, picked the basket where they have put all the vegetables and began to run away with it! Blessing and her mother screamed at the monkey to stop but it kept running, flinging all the vegetables around. When the basket was emptied, it flung it into the bush and climbed to the top of a tree.

Blessing and her mother had to pick the vegetables one after the other. When they finished, her mother asked; "do you want to rest again?"

Blessing cried out, "Let's go home! I can't stand the monkey throwing the vegetables away the second time." Her mother laughed and said, "we'll have been home by now if not for you."

They went home. Since that day, Blessing never think of resting after working until she gets home

COMPREHENSION TEST
1. What did you learn in Proverbs 30:25 - 28?
2. What did you learn in the story?
3. What is the meaning of (i) stiff (ii) fling (iii) delay?
4. Close your book and sing the song about vegetable.

Letter W w

W is for Woman

colour the woman and her son

RHYME ABOUT WOMAN

W is for woman
Who is full of love
She married a man
Who is called Love.

SINGING BIRD WANTS TO TEACH YOU A SONG ABOUT WOMAN

Sorry, I don't have a tune for my song. Would you give it a tune, please? Before you do that, colour me with green, black and orange.

A woman should praise the Lord
Hallelujah!
Her husband should praise the Lord.
Hallelujah!
Her children should praise the Lord
Hallelujah!
Praise the Lord
Hallelujah!

MEMORIZE THIS:

Never fail to keep the promise you make.

LESSON NOTES IN THE STORY BELOW

1. Children of God must always pray about their problems instead of complaining. (Ephisians 6:18)
2. Children of God must not be tired of praying. (1 Thessalonians 5:17, Luke 1:8)
3. God always answers prayers. (Psalm 143:1)

"THE BARREN WOMAN"

There was a woman in the Bible called Hannah. For many years she had no child. Her husband had another woman who had children.

The second woman used to laugh at Hannah because she did not have any child. This made her very sad. Her husband tried to make her happy by giving her many things including plenty of meat but Hannah was always full of tears.

One day, she went to pray in the temple which was like a church at that time. She told God that she wanted a child. "If you give me a child," she said to God, "he would be your servant."

As she was praying, the priest who was like a Pastor then saw her mouth moving. He asked, "Why do you get yourself drunk?"

" I am not drunk sir," Hannah said. "I am only asking God to give me a child."

"Let it be as you have prayed," the priest said.

Hannah later gave birth to a baby boy who later became a prophet of God called Samuel.

Hannah gave birth to more children because she kept the promise she made to God.

COMPREHENSION TEST
1. What did you learn in the story about Hannah?
2. Why did the Priest ask Hannah why she was drunk?
3. Why do you think God gave Hannah more children?

Letter X x

X is for Xylophone

Make this xylophone very colourful

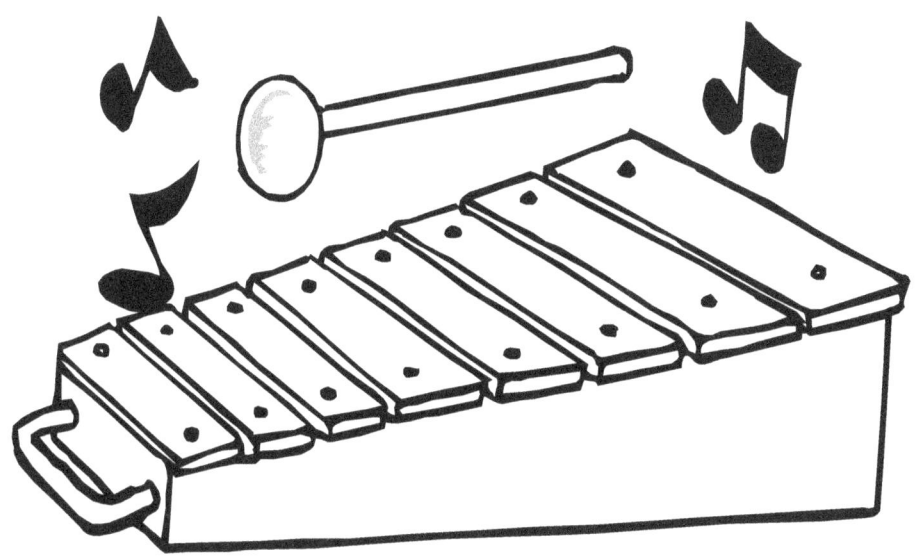

RHYME ABOUT XYLOPHONE

X is for xylophone
The instrument of songs
Songs can be telephone
To talk to God as sons.

SINGING BIRD WANTS TO TEACH YOU A SONG ABOUT MOUNTAIN

My song needs the tune of the song titled "every living soul praise the Lord." You can sing it.

Every xylophone
Every xylophone praise the Lord }2ce
The most high reigneth }3ce
In my life today.

MEMORIZE THIS:
Working harder always bring better results.

LESSON NOTES IN THE STORY BELOW
1. There must be faith and works before there can be results. (James 2:26)
2. To work harder always bring better result. (2Timothy 3:17)
3. Without diligence in works, there cannot be promotion. (Proverb 22:29)

BEN AND THE XYLOPHONE

Ben was a child of God who loved to sing songs of praises. He told his father to buy him a xylophone.

His father said, "well, I've been thinking of making you to improve on your studies in the school. So if you take between first and tenth position in your class during the examination, I'll buy you the xylophone. If you can't, I won't buy it." Ben thought about this for a long time. He knew if he wanted that leading position in the class, he would have to study very hard. There were many brilliant students who equally wanted the position. That was why his position in the class was always between fifteenth and twenty-fifth.

Ben studied as hard as he could before the examination. So when the result came out, he came with twelfth position, which was the best he had ever had so far. All his friends expected him to be happy. Of course, he was not, because that was not the position his father wanted. He knew he would not get any xylophone. He would have to try again next term. Perhaps he would come up with better result in the next examination.

When he got home, he sadly gave the result to his father who smiled and said, "Well, you have a good result but not good enough to get you a xylophone."

"Yes, I know, " Ben said "I'll try again next term."

Guess what happened. His father bought him the xylophone! Ben was so happy that he promised his father he would always do his best.

COMPREHENSION TEST
1. What did you learn in the story about Ben?
2. Why do you think Ben's father bought him the xylophone?
3. Recite or sing the song about xylophone.
4. Close your book and sing the song about xylophone.

Letter Y y

Y is for Youngster

Trace and colour these youngsters

RHYME ABOUT YOUNGSTER

Y is for youngster
Who will be a star
He shines in the dark
For bearing God's mark

SINGING BIRD WANTS TO TEACH YOU A SONG ABOUT YOUNGSTER

> Sorry, I don't have a tune for my song. Would you kindly give it a tune? Before you do that, colour me with blue, yellow and red.

Youngster, go matching in
After living your life for Jesus
To the place God made for you

MEMORIZE THIS:
You can break the most stony hearted person with love.

LESSON NOTES IN THE STORY BELOW

1. A wicked person has no hope except he accepts Jesus into his life. (Proverbs 11:7)
2. The wicked person always get into trouble. (Proverb 28:1)
3. God always favors His children. (Proverb 12:2)

THE TWO YOUNGSTERS

There were two youngsters called Andy and Wala. Andy was a very gentle and obedient youngster who loved God while Wala was very mean and stubborn.

Wala fought in the school and at home. This made many people to run from him. Andy has many friends because he always told everybody about Jesus. Because everybody loved Andy, Wala hated him. So one day, he took a catapult and a stone, hid in a bush and fired it at Andy. The stone hit Andy on the head and all his friends looked around the bush for the person who hurt him. They found Wala and took him to the principal. The principal sent Wala out of school.

Some years later, Andy became a medical doctor. Wala became so poor that he became a street beggar.

One day, while Andy was driving his beautiful car to the office, he saw Wala dying of hunger in the street. He quickly went to carry and take him to the hospital in his car. He gave him food and treated him. Soon, Wala became well.

Andy asked Wala, "do you know me?"

"No, sir," Wala said, "but I know you are a good man for saving my life, sir."

Andy told him whom he was. Suddenly Wala began to cry. Andy told him if he gave his life to Christ, God would forgive him all he had done wrong. Andy became born-again that day. He too became transformed. He was grateful to Andy who helped him to find the Lord.

COMPREHENSION TEST
1. What did you learn in the story Andy and Wala?
2. Why do you think the principal sent Wala out of school?
3. According to Ezekiel 33:7-9, what does God tells us to do about sinners?
4. Close your book and recite the rhyme.

Letter Z z
Z is for Zebra

Can you make this young zebra colourful?

RHYME ABOUT ZEBRA
Z is for Zebra
The horse replica
Created by the Word
The word of God

LESSON NOTES IN THE STORY BELOW
1. God always supplies all the needs of His children. (Philippians 4:19)
2. God never fails those who trust in Him. (Psalm 37:5)
3. Through the Spirit of God, Christians can do what seems impossible to do. (Zechariah 4:6)

THE MISSING ZEBRA

There was once a child of God called Niyi. His parents were poor but he always prayed and praised God every time because he had been taught in the church to always give thanks to God for everything.

One day, all the children in the church were told to ask their parents to give them the money they would need for the camp meeting which was organized for young ones in another town.

Niyi told his parents about it but they didn't have any money to give to him. He became very sad. So he talked to God about it in his prayer.

A few days before the camp meeting, he read about a Zebra that was missing in the zoo. It was announced that anybody that found the Zebra would be given some money.

Niyi did not think about the Zebra until he dreamt that he found the Zebra. He thought he was too young to find a big and wild animal like a Zebra until he read about David and Goliath in the Bible.

Two days before it was time for the meeting, Niyi went to fetch some water at the river and found the Zebra stuck in a muddy area. He quickly went to call the Zookeeper who took it back to the Zoo and gave Niyi the prize money. Niyi happily went to give the money to his parents who gave him some of it for the camp meeting.

COMPREHENSION TEST
1. What did you learn in the story about Niyi?
2. What did you learn in I Samuel 17: 42-50?
3. Why do you think Niyi went to give the money to his parent?
4. Close your book and sing the song about zebra

CHECK OUT OTHER BOOKS BY DIPO TOBY ALAKIJA
Each Serves Either As Edifying Or Evangelical Or Missionary Or Academic Tool At Home, School, Bible Clubs, Sunday Schools, Church, Office And Other Fellowships

NETWORK BIBLE CLUB
YOUTH AND ADULT BOOK ONE
ISBN: 978 - 978- 49874-9-X ISBN: 978-978-49874-9-3

A collection of 26 life transforming stories, 26 poems, 26 hymn tuned songs and weekly Bible lessons

The issue of moral instructions In schools and at homes is threatened with extinction. Consequently, so many youths are involved in prostitution, drug addictions, cultism, fraudulent practices, armed robberies and other crimes. Those who are supposed to be trained as leaders in various walks of life are the ones posing serious threats to many lives. Many parents who fail to add moral values to the upbringing of their children often times breed potential criminals under their roofs without knowing it. Apart from these, many other people negatively influence young ones through the media, music, publications, films, conduct and foul language; making them to lose their moral and family values.

This book one just like the rest of other volumes is an attempt to bring back moral instructions into schools and campuses through the use of stories, hymn tuned songs, poems, Bible lessons and class activities. It is designed to assist teachers and ministers in Secondary Schools, Bible Clubs, Churches and Campus Fellowships to teach people, especially youths the Word of God and serves as a school text book in subjects relating to literature, music and other creative works.

FOOTSTEPS IN THE MUD
ISBN: 978-36348-9-5 ISBN: 978-978-36348-9-3

The Drama Package Of Results Of Research Works That trace Global And Societal Vices To The Corrupt Or Lost Of Family Values

The 13-Episode drama book involves Bosede who learnt many wrong things from her parents' conduct and foul language. She was forced to marry Kola when she became pregnant. Using her mother's method to handle her father, she tried to subject Kola to her control. In the course of that, she made life terrible for him. Although her mother tried to warn her of the implications of maltreating her husband but Bosede has grown out of control. Consequently, while looking for peace, Kola was pushed out of the house. He made friends with some guys who taught him the unholy ways of life and influenced him to become a menace in the house.

Junior who was born at time the couple never proved to be responsible parents also learnt wrong things from them. He decided to follow his father's footsteps by taking alcohol when he was in primary school. As if that was not bad enough, he tried to teach other children in the school the madness in his home. A school teacher, however, was able to influence him and his mother by teaching them Christian morals. Even then, Junior was soon caught in the crossfire at home as his father tried to enlist him as a future member of a secret cult that posed as a social club.

NO MORE TEARS TO SHED
ISBN: 978-49874-3-0 ISBN: 978-978-74-3-1

Kidnappers took Tokunbo away from his grand parents in a city in Nigeria when he was a little boy. A nice woman found him in another town and gave him a false identity. She spoilt him with love, making him to grow into a rebellious teenager that was not appreciated anywhere. When Janet made him a Christian, however, life began to make sense to him until the day he was beaten to the point of death for the offence he knew nothing about. He left the town for the city which, unknown to him, held his true identity and the link to his parents in the United States. To find them was only a question of time.

THE UNROMANTIC LOVE BIRDS
ISBN: 978-4987-5-7 ISBN: 978-978-4974-5-5

And other short stories about love and marriages

They were very much in love right from their school days but when they got married and had children, romance became the game Charles' wife refused to play. No matter how much he tried to make her understand the unbearable condition her unromantic attitude has subjected him into, she would not change. Consequently, after enduring for so long, he was forced to look for the women that would make up for her weakness. He unofficially married a beautiful lady of insane jealousy. Though she was ready to give him what was missing in his marriage, it soon dawn on him that he has solved one big problem only to create a bigger one.

THE BATTLE OF THE CONQUERORS
ISBN: 978-49874-7-3 ISBN: ISBN: 978-978-49874-0-7-9

Wickedness takes over the land of Bondage from First Couple and subjects everybody into slavery without giving anybody the chance to be free. Love brings The Redeemer from Eternity and offers the slaves the chance to escape. Wickedness soon declares war and engages everyone in the battle. The Redeemer makes the redeemed people Conquerors by giving them the armour of war and Comforter but

Wickedness cannot be undone. He has several thousands of years of experience in the war. So he is quick to recognize the weakness of the redeemed people who are ignorant of their strengths and advantages. Although the Conquerors fight like immutable giants, rescuing victims of war, many people suffer heavy casualties.

Since King Wickedness knows that a redeemed person is strong enough to chase one thousand of his warriors at a time, and two would put ten thousand into flight, he enlists as one of his warriors the people's deadliest enemy called Disunity.

Wickedness is able to strike the people by making them to fight with one another, turning what is supposed to be their best moments in the battle into tales of woes.

BLOODSHED IN CAMPUS
ISBN: 978-07350-3-8 ISBN: 978-978-07350-3-6

A poor widow tearfully warned her son, Richard, against joining the bad wagon when he got an admission into one of the Nigerian Universities. He resisted the membership of groups of students, including the Christian Fellowship until he had an encounter with a member of The Black Skulls - a deadly and ruthless secret cult on the campus.

Before Richard knew what he was up against, the head of The Black Skulls had arranged items for his initiation into the cult. While resisting being initiated, he ran to the Christian Fellowship for help. The leader of the Christian Fellowship dragged The President of Students' Union Government (S.U.G) into the conflict. With the involvement of the S.U.G President, another formidable cult called The Red Eyes felt obliged to team up against The Black Skulls. Then the campus turned into a battlefield and BLOODSHED became the order of the black day.

RANSOM FOR LOVE
ISBN: 978-49874-8-1 ISBN: 978-978-4987-4-8-6

She accepted his marriage proposal without knowing the kind of person he was. She soon discovered that he was a mean and ruthless guy who was always ready to get whatever he wanted by all means even if he has to pay for it with the lives of others. She was in his bondage, especially when her parents who believed he was a generous and gentleman were on his side.

Because she considered the proposal to marry him as a marriage engagement with the devil incarnate, she decided that she would rather die than to share her life with him. Then out of the blues, this passionate gentleman sneaked into her life despite all she did to discourage him. She could not resist his love for her when he offered to set her free from the devil incarnate. Then the battle began – sooner than they anticipated.

THE WEIGHT OF DEATH
ISBN: 9978-36348-0-1 ISBN: 978-978-36348-0-0
(Story Of The Spirit Eyes Series)

PLAY ONE: HORROR IN THE FAMILY: Talimi probably did not envisage his death when he was trying to compel his son, Damola to succeed him in the occult Brotherhood. Other members of the secret cult were aware of the battle between them. So when Talimi died; his family, especially Damola who was a diehard Christian began to fall prey to the cult. Using all their powers and the spirit that posed as Talimi's ghost, the cult waged war against the family, tormenting and making them to be at loggerheads.

PLAY TWO: RITUAL KIDS' KIDNAPPERS: Victor and the rest of the members of the School Bible Club were taught that there are lots of evil people in this world but he did not understand why God allowed him to be among the children that were taken away from their parents. He soon understood that he was to be used by God to rescue other children who did not know that everyone that truly believes in Jesus has the power to overcome evil.

PLAY THREE: THE WEIGHT OF DEATH: Awoseun would not have known the real source of problems of mankind if his father had not given him the power to see demons tormenting the people in different ways. What he was yet to know, however, was the power of light over darkness. When he was caught in crossfire between these powers, he desperately sought for deliverance.

SUCCESSFUL CHRISTIANITY AND BASIC MINISTRIES
ISBN: 978-49874-6-0

A Collection Of Resource Materials That Precedes Christian Ministries And Basic Leadership Course Book

The first question is how Christianity is practiced even in a hostile environment. Next to that is the question about the potentials of

Christians in spite of their apparent limitations. The other issues are connected to the successes, deliverance, callings, basic ministries of all Christians and evangelism. Various schools of thoughts have attempted these questions but many answers only portray Christianity as a form of religion instead of a way of life as specified by God. Some answers give room for compromise, hypocrisies, dogmas and denominational doctrines. The misconceptions about these areas of Christianity have brought about worldliness instead of righteousness and false achievements instead of fulfillment.

This book which contains six different subjects had been used to hold seminars at various levels, train ministers and Christian workers in Bible Schools and to equip the Church. It explains in simple terms the seemingly complex issues on practice of Christianity, Potentials, Deliverance, God's Kind Of Success, Evangelism and Basic Ministries of a Christian with Biblical principles, life transforming stories and illustrations.

CHRISTIAN MINISTRIES AND BASIC LEADERSHIP
ISBN: 978-36348-7-9 ISBN: 978-978-36348-7-9
A Collection Of Resource Materials That Follows Up Successful Christianity And Basic Ministries Course Book

As it is common to say that the hood does not make a monk, the dignified positions and bogus titles of many Christian leaders in modern days do not really make them Gospel Ministers.

This course book - a compilation of five resource materials on Missions And Outreach Ministries, Christian Communication Arts, Christian Leadership, Christian Education Methodology and Ministries Of Improvisations - aims at making every matured Christian an effective minister and leader at their respective homes, communities and nations. It teaches various ways Christians can communicate the word of God, meeting up to their responsibilities as ministers and leaders that reconcile people to God, edifying the Body Of Christ and reaching out to souls at the same time.

All of the resource materials are in use in Bible Schools like College Of Christian Education And Missions, in Churches and other ministries to raise Christian workers, Evangelists, Missionaries and other Ministers that serve at various levels and leadership capacities.

CHRISTIAN MINISTRIES AND BASIC LEADERSHIP
ISBN: 978-36348-7-9 ISBN: 978-978-36348-7-9
A Collection Of Resource Materials That Follows Up Successful Christianity And Basic Ministries Course Book

As it is common to say that the hood does not make a monk, the dignified positions and bogus titles of many Christian leaders in modern days do not really make them Gospel Ministers.

This course book - a compilation of five resource materials on Missions And Outreach Ministries, Christian Communication Arts, Christian Leadership, Christian Education Methodology and Ministries Of Improvisations - aims at making every matured Christian an effective minister and leader at their respective homes, communities and nations. It teaches various ways Christians can communicate the word of God, meeting up to their responsibilities as ministers and leaders that reconcile people to God, edifying the Body Of Christ and reaching out to souls at the same time.

All of the resource materials are in use in Bible Schools like College Of Christian Education And Missions, in Churches and other ministries to raise Christian workers, Evangelists, Missionaries and other Ministers that serve at various levels and leadership capacities.

INSANITY OF HUMANITY
ISBN: 978-36348-6-0 ISBN: 978-978-36348-6-2
The Results Of Research Works Into Various Methods Of Brainwashing

Man is made to exercise his freewill. The mind of his own and the power to choose between right and wrong, good and evil, light and darkness is about to be washed away through brainwashing. The agents of control dubbed as Secret Government by John Todd (the top Illuninati defector) have put necessary machinery in place to ensure that all human beings are in conformity in their thinking and ways of life, trying to wipe away diversity, which makes each person unique.

This book attempts to shed light on how the techniques of mind control are applied through the use of propaganda, education, entertainments, drugs, religions, media and other means of communications. It is the result of research works, some of which are based on findings of various researchers and writers like Bugger Lugz, Edward Hunter, Hadley Cantril, Herbert Krugman, David L. Robb, Vaughan Bell, Juliana Gomez, Ryan Duffy Vice, Henry Makow, David Nicholls, Fritz Springmeire, Steven Hassan, Renate Thienel, Debra Pursell, Mary Pride and a host of others who are acknowledged in this book.

CALVARY ROCK RESOURCE BOOKLETS
ISSN: 1595 93X

The Quarterly Missionary Booklets That Are Designed To Teach Children, Youths And Adults In Schools, Fellowships, Churches, At Homes, Office And Other Places.

Although all the various volumes of this booklet can be used independently of other books but it is recommended that it should be used as part of supplementary materials to make up for Foundation and Network Bible Club Story Books for both children and adults in School, Church, Campus, Office and other Fellowships.

Each of the volume is rich with quarterly Bible lessons, stories, drama, songs, seminar, tract materials and a host of other things that can be used to edify, educate, entertains and evangelize every category of people, ranging from children to elderly persons.

Every volume is designed to equip school teachers, ministers in Churches or campus or office fellowships and other people who wish to work with the Lord.

All These And Other Books Are Distributed Worldwide And Published By The Publishing House Of Calvary Rock Resources

*Ikenne-Remo, Nigeria
*Manchester, United Kingdom
*New York, United States

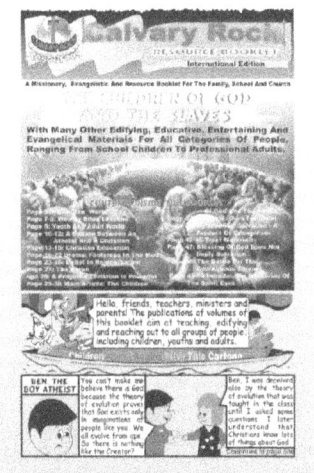

www.calvaryrock.org

www.ingramcontent.com/pod-product-compliance
Lightning Source LLC
Chambersburg PA
CBHW020009050426
42450CB00005B/388